Jean Piaget's Theory of Cognitive Development: A Simple Guide

Dr. Milos Kankaras

Published by Dr. Milos Kankaras, 2023.

While every precaution has been taken in the preparation of this book, the publisher assumes no responsibility for errors or omissions, or for damages resulting from the use of the information contained herein.

JEAN PIAGET'S THEORY OF COGNITIVE DEVELOPMENT: A SIMPLE GUIDE

First edition. June 16, 2023.

Copyright © 2023 Dr. Milos Kankaras.

ISBN: 979-8223049340

Written by Dr. Milos Kankaras.

Table of Contents

Piaget's Theory of Cognitive Development: A Simple Guide

Chapter 1: Introduction to Jean Piaget's Theory of Development

1.1 Background on Piaget

Jean Piaget was a Swiss psychologist and philosopher who is widely known for his comprehensive and influential theory of cognitive development. Born in 1896, Piaget spent much of his career observing and studying children, seeking to understand the ways in which they make sense of the world around them. Through his research, Piaget developed a comprehensive theory of cognitive development that has been widely accepted and used as a framework for understanding how children think, learn, a////nd grow.

Piaget was born in Neuchâtel, Switzerland, where he spent much of his childhood exploring the natural world and observing the behavior of other children. He later studied biology at the University of Neuchâtel, where he became interested in the ways in which animals learn and adapt to their environments. This early interest in learning and adaptation eventually led Piaget to study psychology, which he pursued at the University of Zurich.

In his early research, Piaget focused on studying how children think and learn. He became interested in how children's cognitive development occurs over time, and how they are able to construct their own knowledge of the world through experience and interaction. Piaget's research on children's development was based on the idea that children are active learners who build their own understanding of the world through their experiences and interactions with the environment. He believed that children actively construct their own understanding of the world, and that this process is driven by the interplay between their experiences and the cognitive structures they have already developed.

1.2 Overview of Piaget's Theory of Cognitive Development

Piaget's theory of cognitive development is a comprehensive framework that provides an explanation of how children develop cognitively from birth to adulthood. The theory outlines four distinct stages of development, each of which is characterized by different patterns of thought and behavior. The four stages of Piaget's theory are: the sensorimotor stage, the preoperational stage, the concrete operational stage, and the formal operational stage.

Throughout each of these stages, Piaget emphasized the importance of the child's active construction of knowledge, as well as the role of experience and interaction with the world in shaping this development. Piaget's theory also highlights the role of schemas, or mental structures that help children organize and make sense of their experiences. Schemas are constantly changing and adapting as children encounter new experiences and information, which helps them to build new and more sophisticated understandings of the world.

The process of equilibration is also a key component of Piaget's theory. Equilibration refers to the process by which children maintain a balance between their current understanding of the world and their experiences. When children encounter new information or experiences that cannot be incorporated into their existing schemas, they must revise their understanding of the world in order to maintain a state of balance. This process of equilibration allows children to build new and more sophisticated understandings of the world, and drives their cognitive development over time.

In addition to describing the stages of cognitive development, Piaget's theory also provides important insights into the development of thought and reasoning, as well as the ways in which children learn and make sense of the world. For example, Piaget's theory highlights the importance of concrete experiences and hands-on activities in helping children to build their understanding of the world. It also emphasizes the importance of allowing children to take an active role in their own learning and discovery, rather than simply imparting information to them.

Overall, Piaget's theory of cognitive development remains one of the most important and widely accepted frameworks for understanding how children develop cognitively and make sense of the world around them. Despite some criticisms of the theory, Piaget's ideas have had a profound impact on the field of psychology, and continue to shape our understanding of child development and learning today.

II. The Four Stages of Cognitive Development

A. Sensorimotor Stage (birth to 2 years)

Description of the stage

The sensory-motor stage is the first of Piaget's four stages of cognitive development, and encompasses the first two years of life. During this stage, infants and toddlers are building a foundation for their later cognitive development, as they explore and make sense of their world through their senses and movements.

During the sensory-motor stage, children are heavily focused on their immediate sensory experiences and physical interactions with the world. They use their five senses - sight, touch, hearing, taste, and smell - to gather information about their surroundings, and engage in repetitive movements and behaviors in order to learn about objects and the relationships between them.

One key aspect of the sensory-motor stage is the development of object permanence, which is the understanding that objects continue to exist even when they are not in sight. Infants initially struggle with this concept, but gradually come to understand that objects continue to exist when they are out of sight. This is an important development, as it lays the foundation for future cognitive processes such as categorization and spatial reasoning.

Another important aspect of the sensory-motor stage is the development of schemas, or mental structures that help children organize their experiences and make sense of the world. Schemas are initially simple and limited, but become increasingly complex and sophisticated as children progress through the sensory-motor stage and into the later stages of development.

During the sensorimotor stage, children also begin to engage in what Piaget referred to as "primary circular reactions." These are repetitive, goal-directed behaviors that are motivated by the pleasure or satisfaction that comes from achieving a specific outcome. For example, an infant might repeatedly shake a rattle in order to produce a desired sound, or engage in repetitive movements in order to explore the properties of an object.

As children progress through the sensory-motor stage, their schemas become more complex and their understanding of the world becomes more sophisticated. They also become capable of engaging in secondary circular reactions, which involve adapting and adjusting their behavior based on their experiences. For example, a child might learn to shake a rattle in different ways in order to produce different sounds, or engage in more complex explorations of objects in order to learn about their properties.

It's important to note that the sensory-motor stage is not limited to infants and toddlers. Even as children enter the later stages of development, they continue to engage in sensory-motor experiences and behaviors that help them to build their understanding of the world. For example, children may engage in hands-on experiences, such as building with blocks or playing with toys, in order to learn about spatial relationships and other important concepts.

Overall, the sensory-motor stage is a critical period in a child's development, as it lays the foundation for future cognitive and intellectual growth. By exploring their world through their senses and movements, children are able to build the schemas and mental structures that will be the foundation for their later understanding of the world.

A real-life examples of typical behaviours in this stage:

A TYPICAL REAL-LIFE example of a child demonstrating object permanence is when they are playing with a toy, such as a ball, and it rolls under a piece of furniture. The child may initially look for the ball where they last saw it, but when it doesn't reappear, they begin to search for it in other locations. They may move furniture or crawl under it, indicating that they understand that the ball still exists even though it is out of sight. This behavior shows that the child has developed an understanding of object permanence, which is the idea that objects continue to exist even when they are not in sight. This is a crucial milestone in a child's cognitive development, as it lays the foundation for later understandings of cause and effect, spatial relationships, and other important concepts.

Advice to parents and carers:

A PARENT SHOULD APPROACH and deal with a child in the sensory-motor stage by providing them with a supportive and stimulating environment that encourages exploration and discovery. According to Piaget's theory of development, children in this stage learn best through hands-on experiences and interactions with their physical surroundings. Therefore, a parent can support their child's development by:

- Providing age-appropriate toys and materials that encourage exploration and discovery, such as blocks, balls, and sensory toys.
- Engaging in play activities that allow the child to use their senses and movements, such as crawling through tunnels, stacking blocks, and playing with balls.
- Encouraging the child to repeat actions and behaviors that bring pleasure or satisfaction, such as shaking a rattle or

stacking blocks.

- Allowing the child to explore and manipulate objects in a safe environment, while also providing appropriate guidance and boundaries.
- Being patient and allowing the child to take the lead in play activities, while also being attentive and responsive to their needs and interests.

It's also important for a parent to keep in mind that the sensory-motor stage is just the beginning of a child's cognitive development, and that they will continue to grow and change as they progress through the later stages of development. By providing a supportive and stimulating environment during the sensory-motor stage, a parent can help lay the foundation for their child's future cognitive, intellectual, and emotional growth.

Key Takeaways on the Sensory-motor Stage:

THE SENSORY-MOTOR STAGE is the first stage of Piaget's theory of cognitive development and lasts from birth to 2 years old.

During this stage, infants build knowledge through interactions with their physical environment and rely on their senses and motor skills to understand the world around them.

Piaget described 6 sub-stages of development during the Sensory-motor stage, each characterized by a different level of development in object permanence, representation and coordination of secondary circular reactions.

This stage is important because it lays the foundation for future cognitive development, as infants form their first mental representations of objects, people, and events.

Piaget's theory has been supported by empirical research, with numerous studies finding that infants exhibit the developmental milestones described by Piaget.

B. Preoperational Stage (2 to 7 years)

Description of the stage

The Preoperational Stage is the second stage of Piaget's theory of cognitive development, and it typically occurs between the ages of 2 and 7 years old. During this stage, children develop a greater understanding of the mental representations of objects, which allows them to think about objects and events symbolically. This stage is characterized by the development of symbolic thought, the use of mental images and symbols to represent objects and events, and the ability to engage in mental manipulation of these symbols.

One of the key features of the preoperational stage is the development of egocentrism, the tendency to view the world from one's own perspective and to believe that others share the same view. This can lead to difficulties in understanding the perspectives of others, which can impact the child's ability to engage in cooperative play and other social activities.

Another key feature of the preoperational stage is the development of semi-permanent concepts, or mental categories, which allow the child to classify objects and events based on certain characteristics. This helps the child to make predictions and understand cause-and-effect relationships, but can also lead to a lack of flexibility in thinking and a tendency to view the world in rigid categories.

One of the most significant changes that occur during the preoperational stage is the development of language and the ability to use symbols to represent objects and events. Children at this stage begin to understand that words can be used to represent objects, and they become increasingly proficient at using language to communicate their thoughts and ideas.

Another important aspect of the preoperational stage is the development of memory and the ability to recall past events. Children at this stage have a better memory for events that are emotionally significant or that involve objects that are meaningful to them. They also become better at recalling sequences of events, which helps them to understand cause-and-effect relationships.

Despite the many advances in cognitive abilities during the preoperational stage, children at this age are still limited by their lack of understanding of mental operations, or the ability to manipulate symbols and mental images. They cannot perform mental transformations, such as reversing the order of events, or imagining what would happen if a certain event did not occur. This can lead to difficulties in understanding complex concepts and problem-solving, which are important skills that will be developed later in life.

To support a child's development during the preoperational stage, it is important to provide them with a rich and stimulating environment that encourages exploration and discovery. This can include providing age-appropriate toys and materials, such as blocks, puzzles, and books, and engaging in activities that encourage the child to use their imagination and to think creatively. It is also important to provide opportunities for the child to engage in cooperative play and other social activities, as this can help them to develop their understanding of the perspectives of others and to improve their social skills.

In conclusion, the preoperational stage is a critical period in a child's cognitive development, as it marks the transition from the concrete and sensory-based understanding of the world to a more abstract and symbolic way of thinking. By providing a supportive and stimulating environment, and by engaging in activities that encourage exploration and discovery, parents and caregivers can help children to make the most of this important stage of development.

A real-life examples of typical behaviours in this stage:

SYMBOLIC THOUGHT: A typical real-life example of a child demonstrating symbolic thought during the preoperational stage is when they use toys or objects to represent other things, such as using a block to symbolize a car.

Egocentrism: A typical real-life example of a child demonstrating egocentrism during the preoperational stage is when they believe that everyone sees the world from their own perspective and assume that others share their views and thoughts. For example, a child may assume that everyone knows what they are thinking without having to say it.

Concept Development: A typical real-life example of a child demonstrating concept development during the preoperational stage is when they categorize objects based on specific characteristics. For example, a child may group all the animals they know into a category called "pets" or "farm animals."

Language: A typical real-life example of a child demonstrating language development during the preoperational stage is when they use words to communicate their thoughts and ideas, even if they may not always use them correctly. For example, a child may ask "Why sky blue?"

Memory: A typical real-life example of a child demonstrating memory development during the preoperational stage is when they have a better memory for emotionally significant events and can recall the sequence of events in a story. For example, a child may remember the details of a favorite book or movie, but have trouble recalling the events of a less interesting story.

Mental Operations: A typical real-life example of a child demonstrating a lack of understanding of mental operations during the preoperational stage is when they have difficulty understanding the concept of conservation. For example, a child may believe that a tall glass of juice contains more juice than a short glass, even if both glasses have the same amount of liquid.

Piaget's Conservation Task

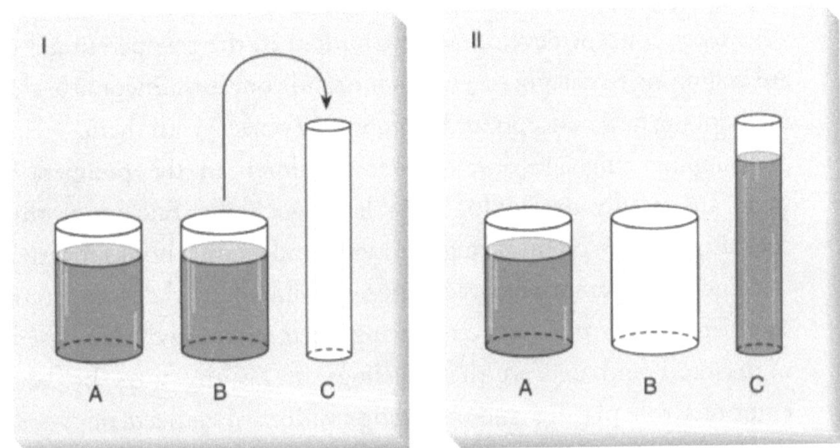

These real-life examples demonstrate the key characteristics of children's behavior during the preoperational stage, as described by Piaget's theory of cognitive development. By understanding these behaviors, parents, teachers, and caregivers can provide a supportive environment that helps children make the most of this important stage of development.

Advice to parents and carers:

HEN DEALING WITH A child in the preoperational stage, it is important for a parent or caregiver to keep in mind Piaget's postulates about this stage of development. Here are a few tips for how to best approach and deal with a child in the preoperational stage:

Encourage symbolic play: Children in the preoperational stage often use toys and objects to represent other things. Encourage this type of play by providing a variety of materials and allowing children to use their imaginations.

Be patient with egocentrism: Children in this stage are still developing their understanding of other people's perspectives, so it's important to be patient with their egocentric behavior. Try to provide opportunities for them to see things from different perspectives, such as by playing games that involve taking turns.

Foster concept development: Children in the preoperational stage are beginning to categorize and understand concepts. Encourage this by introducing new concepts and categorizing objects with them.

Support language development: Children in the preoperational stage are rapidly developing their language skills. Encourage this by speaking to them often, asking questions, and reading books together.

Encourage emotional regulation: Children in the preoperational stage may have difficulty regulating their emotions. Help them to understand and express their feelings in healthy ways by labeling emotions, role-playing, and providing comfort when needed.

Promote mental operations: Children in this stage are beginning to understand mental operations, but they may still struggle with concepts like conservation. Provide opportunities for them to practice their mental operations, such as by doing simple puzzles or counting objects.

By following these tips, parents and caregivers can provide a supportive environment that fosters healthy development during the preoperational stage. Understanding Piaget's postulates about this stage can help them create activities and experiences that encourage children to grow and develop to their full potential.

Key Takeaways on the Preoperational Stage:

AGE RANGE: THIS STAGE occurs between the ages of 2 to 7 years old.

Symbolic Thought: Children develop the ability to think symbolically, using mental images and symbols to represent objects and events.

Egocentrism: Children develop egocentrism, the tendency to view the world from their own perspective and believe others share the same view.

Concept Development: Children develop semi-permanent concepts or mental categories to classify objects and events based on certain characteristics.

Language: Children develop language and become proficient at using words to communicate their thoughts and ideas.

Memory: Children have a better memory for emotionally significant events and become better at recalling sequences of events.

Mental Operations: Children are limited by their lack of understanding of mental operations and cannot perform mental transformations.

Stimulating Environment: To support a child's development during this stage, it is important to provide a rich and stimulating environment that encourages exploration and discovery.

Social Skills: Engaging in cooperative play and other social activities can help children develop their understanding of others' perspectives and improve their social skills.

In summary, the preoperational stage is a critical period in a child's cognitive development, marking the transition from a concrete to a more abstract way of thinking. By providing a supportive environment and engaging in activities that encourage exploration and discovery, parents and caregivers can help children make the most of this important stage.

C. Concrete Operational Stage (7 to 12 years)

Description of the stage

The Concrete Operational Stage is the third stage of Jean Piaget's theory of cognitive development. During this stage, children typically develop the ability to think logically about concrete events and objects. This stage occurs from approximately 7 to 11 years of age and is marked by a significant increase in children's cognitive abilities and their ability to understand and solve problems in their environment.

Conservation

CONSERVATION REFERS to the understanding that certain physical attributes of an object remain unchanged despite alterations in its appearance. In the Concrete Operational stage of development, children gain the ability to conserve through cognitive operations. This means that they can mentally manipulate information and preserve the value of a physical characteristic despite changes in its appearance.

One of the most famous examples of conservation is the liquid conservation task, in which children are presented with two identical glasses filled with the same amount of liquid. The liquid from one glass is then transferred to a taller and skinnier glass, and the child is asked if the two glasses still contain the same amount of liquid. Before reaching the Concrete Operational stage, children typically believe that the taller glass contains more liquid because it looks larger. However, children in the Concrete Operational stage are able to understand that the quantity of the liquid remains unchanged despite changes in its appearance.

Another example of conservation is the conservation of mass. Children in the Concrete Operational stage understand that the amount of matter in an object remains the same, even if the object is reshaped or resized. For example, if a child is shown two balls of playdough, one larger and one smaller, they are able to understand that both balls contain the same amount of playdough even though one is larger.

Conservation is a critical aspect of cognitive development and is an important step in the development of logic and reasoning. It demonstrates that children are able to mentally manipulate information and understand that certain physical properties of an object remain constant despite changes in its appearance. As children continue to develop and reach the formal operational stage, they will be able to apply this understanding of conservation to more abstract concepts, such as time, volume, and number.

Seriation

SERIATION REFERS TO the ability to arrange objects in a logical sequence based on size, shape, weight, or other attributes. It involves the development of an organized and systematic way of thinking.

Seriation is an important step towards the development of more advanced mathematical skills such as counting, measuring, and arithmetic. Children in the concrete operational stage learn to put objects in order, categorize them and make comparisons based on various attributes. For example, they can arrange blocks in size order, sort toy animals by type, or categorize their toys based on color.

Seriation also involves the development of a sense of scale and perspective, allowing children to understand how objects relate to each other in size, height, and distance. This ability helps children to understand how to use tools, such as measuring tapes, to compare and make quantitative assessments.

In addition to being a critical component of mathematical development, seriation also plays a role in other areas such as language development, social and emotional development, and problem solving. For example, children who have developed seriation skills can use their understanding of the relationship between objects to make predictions and understand cause-and-effect relationships.

Transitivity

TRANSITIVITY IS AN important concept in Jean Piaget's theory of cognitive development, and refers to the child's ability to logically order and connect events or objects in a meaningful sequence. During the concrete operational stage, children develop the capacity for transitive reasoning, which allows them to understand the relationships between objects and events based on their attributes, such as size, weight, or quantity.

Transitivity is the foundation for the child's ability to make inferences, draw conclusions, and solve problems in a systematic and rational manner. For example, a child can understand that if A is bigger than B and B is bigger than C, then A must be bigger than C. This ability to deduce relationships between objects or events based on attributes is a crucial step in the child's development towards abstract thinking and reasoning.

Transitive reasoning also plays a role in the child's ability to understand mathematical concepts, such as addition, subtraction, and multiplication. For instance, a child can understand that if two groups of objects have the same total number, then one group can be divided into smaller parts to create the other group.

Reversibility

REVERSIBILITY IS A key characteristic of the concrete operational stage in Jean Piaget's theory of cognitive development. Reversibility refers to the child's ability to understand that actions can be reversed, which leads to an understanding of cause and effect relationships.

During the concrete operational stage, children develop the capacity for reversibility, which allows them to understand that operations can be undone. For example, if a child pours water from a tall glass into a short glass, they understand that the water can be poured back into the tall glass. This capacity for reversibility is crucial in helping children develop an understanding of the causal relationships between events and objects, and enables them to engage in mental operations and problem solving.

Reversibility also helps children understand the effects of their actions on the world around them. For instance, a child can understand that if they take a toy away from a sibling, the sibling will no longer have the toy. This is a significant step in the child's development towards moral reasoning and understanding of social rules.

Reversibility is closely related to the development of mental manipulation skills, as children learn to mentally manipulate objects and events in their mind, and reverse the operations to see the potential outcomes. This ability to manipulate information mentally is crucial for higher-level thinking skills, such as hypothetical reasoning and mental simulation.

Class inclusion

CLASS INCLUSION IS a cognitive process that occurs during the Concrete Operational stage of development, according to Piaget's theory. It involves the ability to understand that a class or group can include smaller subgroups, and that these subgroups are still a part of the larger class. This ability is an important aspect of the child's developing logical thinking and allows them to understand more complex relationships between objects and ideas.

For example, a child who understands class inclusion knows that a bird is a part of the class of "animals," even though it is also a part of the subgroup of "feathered animals." They understand that these two categories are not mutually exclusive and that the smaller subgroup is still a part of the larger class. This cognitive ability helps children understand that different things can belong to multiple categories at the same time.

Decentration

DECENTRATION REFERS to the ability of a child to consider multiple aspects of a problem or task at the same time during the Concrete Operational stage. This ability allows children to think more logically and systematically, and is a crucial development in their cognitive abilities.

During the Concrete Operational stage, children develop the ability to decentrate, which means they can take into account multiple aspects of a problem or task. This ability allows children to move beyond the egocentric thinking of the Preoperational stage and to start considering different perspectives and information. For example, a child may be able to consider multiple variables when solving a mathematical problem, or may be able to consider multiple aspects of a situation when making a decision.

Decentration is an important step in the development of children's cognitive abilities, as it allows them to start thinking more logically and systematically. This ability is necessary for children to understand complex concepts and to solve problems that involve multiple variables. In addition, decentration helps children to understand relationships between objects and events, and to see how changes in one variable may affect other variables.

Children during the Concrete Operational Stage also develop the ability to use logical reasoning and systematic problem solving to solve concrete problems. They are able to use the process of elimination to solve problems and make predictions based on past experiences. This increased ability to reason logically allows children to engage in more complex problem solving and planning activities.

Main limitations of child's thinking in this stage

HOWEVER, DESPITE THE advances made during this stage, there are still several limitations in children's thinking. Some of these limitations include:

Lack of Abstract Reasoning: Children in the Concrete Operational Stage are not yet capable of abstract reasoning and tend to have difficulty understanding concepts that are not tangible or concrete.

Difficulty with Hypotheticals: Children in this stage also struggle with hypothetical or theoretical situations as they prefer to focus on tangible objects and real-life experiences.

Limited Mental Manipulation: Children in the Concrete Operational Stage have limited mental manipulation skills and tend to have difficulty visualizing and manipulating objects in their minds.

The rigidity of Thinking: Children in this stage can become rigid in their thinking, meaning that they tend to stick to familiar perspectives and are resistant to change.

Limited Understanding of Probability: Children in the Concrete Operational Stage have a limited understanding of probability and often have difficulty with complex mathematical concepts.

Egocentrism: Children in this stage are still egocentric, meaning that they tend to focus on their own perspectives and struggle to understand the perspectives of others.

Lack of Logical Reasoning: Children in the Concrete Operational Stage tend to have limited logical reasoning skills and can struggle with deductive and inductive reasoning.

Limited Understanding of Conservation: Despite their ability to understand conservation in some areas, children in this stage often struggle with understanding conservation in other areas such as quantity, weight, and volume.

Difficulty with Inferred Properties: Children in this stage often struggle with inferring the properties of objects and tend to focus on the physical characteristics of objects rather than the underlying properties that make them what they are.

A real-life examples of typical behaviours in this stage:

CONSERVATION: A 7-YEAR-old child is playing with blocks, stacking them up to make a tower. When their friend comes over and adds a block to the top, the child immediately becomes upset. They argue that their tower is now taller and not the same as it was before. This behavior shows the child's understanding of conservation, as they recognize that the quantity of blocks hasn't changed despite its appearance.

Seriation: A 9-year-old child is playing with a set of blocks of different sizes. They start by arranging them in order of size from smallest to largest, then switch to largest to smallest. This demonstrates their understanding of seriation, as they are able to organize objects based on their physical attributes.

Transitivity: A 6-year-old child is playing with marbles and is asked to choose which marble is the biggest. They choose one and then another. When asked which is bigger, they are able to consistently choose the larger one. This behavior shows the child's understanding of transitivity, as they are able to compare and order objects based on their attributes.

Reversibility: A 8-year-old child is playing with building blocks and creates a structure that they can no longer see. They begin to take the structure apart and rebuild it in reverse, demonstrating their understanding of reversibility. They understand that they can undo their actions and change their structure back to its original form.

Class Inclusion: A 7-year-old child is asked to group objects into categories, such as "fruit" and "vegetables". When asked why a tomato is a vegetable, they explain that it is a type of fruit. This behavior shows the child's understanding of class inclusion, as they understand that objects can belong to more than one category based on their attributes.

Decentration: A 9-year-old child is playing with a puzzle and is able to take multiple elements into consideration when solving it. They are able to move pieces around and consider different options, demonstrating their understanding of decentration. They are able to think about multiple aspects of a problem and keep track of multiple pieces of information.

Advice to parents and carers:

A TEACHER IN THE CONCRETE Operational stage should approach their students with hands-on, interactive activities and lessons. Children in this stage are actively exploring and experimenting, so it is important to provide them with opportunities to manipulate materials and engage in practical problem-solving. Teachers can utilize the child's growing understanding of conservation, seriation, and transitivity to help guide their learning and facilitate their growth in these areas.

For example, a teacher can encourage the child's understanding of conservation through hands-on activities, such as pouring water from one container to another of different shapes, to demonstrate the concept that the amount of water remains the same, regardless of its container. A teacher can also help a child understand seriation by sorting objects based on their size, color, or shape. Through these hands-on activities, the child can build their understanding of how to logically order and categorize objects.

In terms of transitivity, teachers can help children understand cause-and-effect relationships by conducting simple experiments, such as dropping balls from different heights to see how it affects their bounce. The child can develop their understanding of how certain actions result in specific outcomes.

Lastly, the teacher can facilitate the child's development of decentration by providing opportunities for them to look at problems from different perspectives. For example, the teacher can encourage children to think about problems from multiple viewpoints during group discussions, or to consider different solutions to a problem when working on a project.

Key Takeaways on the Concrete Operational Stage:

THE CONCRETE OPERATIONAL Stage is a crucial stage in a child's cognitive development, characterized by the development of logic and the ability to think systematically. Here are the key takeaways on the Concrete Operational Stage:

- Development of logic: Children in the concrete operational stage develop the ability to think logically and systematically, which allows them to solve problems in a systematic and orderly manner.
- Conservation: Children in this stage begin to understand the concept of conservation, which refers to the principle that a substance remains the same even if its appearance changes.
- Reversibility: Children in the concrete operational stage understand that operations can be reversed, which allows them to understand cause and effect.
- Class inclusion: Children in this stage are able to categorize

objects into groups and understand the relationships between them.

- Decentration: Children in the concrete operational stage are able to consider multiple aspects of a problem at once, which is known as decentration.
- Mental operations: Children in the concrete operational stage are able to perform mental operations, such as adding and subtracting, in their minds.

Overall, the Concrete Operational Stage is a crucial stage in a child's cognitive development, as it marks the development of key cognitive skills that are necessary for later stages of development. Understanding the key takeaways of this stage can help parents and educators support children's cognitive growth and development.

D. Formal Operational Stage (12 years and up)

Description of the stage

The Formal Operational Stage is the fourth and final stage of Jean Piaget's theory of cognitive development. It is characterized by the development of abstract thinking and logical reasoning. Children in this stage are capable of formal thought processes, which allows them to manipulate abstract concepts and think about hypothetical situations.

In the Formal Operational Stage, children are able to develop a more sophisticated understanding of the world around them. They are able to consider multiple perspectives and possibilities, which leads to an increased ability to think critically and logically. This stage is marked by the development of systematic, structured and abstract thinking.

Logical and systematical thinking

THE ABILITY TO THINK logically and systematically is a hallmark of the Formal Operational stage in Jean Piaget's theory of cognitive development. This stage is marked by the ability to think logically and systematically about abstract concepts, making it possible for individuals to develop a clear and well-structured understanding of the world around them.

During this stage, individuals are able to engage in mental operations, which are mental processes that allow for the manipulation of abstract ideas and symbols. These mental operations include abstract reasoning, systematic problem solving, and logical deduction. With these abilities, individuals can develop a sophisticated understanding of complex concepts, such as cause and effect, cause-and-effect relationships, and deductive reasoning.

In the Formal Operational stage, individuals are able to generate hypotheses and test them through systematic and logical deduction. They can also engage in hypothetical reasoning, where they consider different possibilities and consequences of a given situation. This ability to think systematically and logically allows individuals to make well-informed decisions, critically evaluate information, and engage in logical problem solving.

Abstact thinking

ABSTRACT THINKING IS a key aspect of the Formal Operational Stage of cognitive development, according to Jean Piaget's theory. In this stage, which typically occurs in late adolescence and early adulthood, individuals are able to think logically and systematically about abstract concepts and ideas, and can engage in hypothetical and deductive reasoning. They are able to think beyond the concrete, observable aspects of a situation, and consider more abstract and theoretical ideas.

Abstract thinking in the Formal Operational Stage allows individuals to develop their own theories, opinions and beliefs based on logic, reason and evidence, rather than relying solely on past experiences and observations. They can engage in critical thinking and evaluate different perspectives, and are able to understand complex concepts and arguments.

In addition to abstract thinking, individuals in the Formal Operational Stage are also able to think about multiple variables and factors at the same time, and can make systematic comparisons and understand cause and effect relationships. They are able to solve complex problems and plan for future events, using logic and deduction to predict outcomes.

This ability to think abstractly and logically about ideas and concepts is essential for academic and intellectual growth, as well as for personal development. It allows individuals to explore and understand the world in new and innovative ways, and helps them to make informed decisions about their lives and future.

Other abilities

THIS STAGE IS ALSO associated with several other key abilities that are crucial for cognitive development. These include:

Hypothetical and deductive reasoning: During this stage, individuals are capable of making predictions about the outcomes of certain events, and formulating hypotheses. They can also apply deductive reasoning to solve problems and make informed decisions.

Conceptualizing: In this stage, individuals are able to form abstract concepts, which can be applied to a wide range of situations and circumstances. They can then use these concepts to organize and categorize information, and understand the world around them.

Scientific reasoning: Piaget believed that the Formal Operational Stage marks the emergence of scientific reasoning. Individuals in this stage are capable of testing hypotheses, analyzing data and drawing conclusions based on evidence.

Reflective thinking: At this stage, individuals are capable of introspection, self-reflection and self-awareness. They can analyze their own thoughts and emotions, and develop a better understanding of themselves and their place in the world.

These key abilities are important milestones in cognitive development, and form the foundation for higher level thinking and problem solving. With the ability to think abstractly, logically and systematically, individuals in the Formal Operational Stage are well equipped to tackle the challenges of adulthood.

A real-life examples of typical behaviours in this stage:

ABILITY TO THINK LOGICALLY About Abstract Concepts: A 15-year-old girl is in a heated debate with her friends about the best way to tackle climate change. She logically lays out several potential solutions, evaluating the pros and cons of each one and explaining her reasoning behind each decision.

Systematic and Logical Thinking: A 12-year-old boy is trying to figure out the best way to spend his allowance money. He sets a budget, lists out all of his options and evaluates each one systematically, using logic to determine which one is the best choice for him.

Abstract Thinking: A 14-year-old boy is writing a paper on the philosophical concept of free will. He is able to understand and articulate complex ideas about determinism and free will, showing an ability to think about abstract concepts in a logical and meaningful way.

Hypothetical Reasoning: A 15-year-old girl is in a science class, and the teacher asks her to think about the implications of a new discovery in the field of genetics. She is able to think critically about the potential consequences of this discovery and engage in hypothetical reasoning about how it may impact society in the future.

Scientific Reasoning: A 13-year-old boy is building a model for a science project. He is able to systematically test different variables to determine which ones have the greatest impact on his experiment, demonstrating a strong ability to engage in scientific reasoning and problem-solving.

Advice to parents and carers:

WHEN WORKING WITH CHILDREN in the Formal Operational stage, it's important for parents and teachers to understand their increased ability to think abstractly and logically. This means that children in this stage are able to think about complex concepts and theories and analyze them systematically.

One way for parents and teachers to engage with children in this stage is to encourage them to think critically and ask questions. This can help them develop their ability to think logically and systematically, as well as challenge their own beliefs and assumptions. By asking open-ended questions and allowing children to come up with their own solutions, they can foster independence and problem-solving skills.

Another approach is to provide real-world problems and scenarios that children can apply their critical thinking skills to. This can help them develop a deeper understanding of abstract concepts and apply them to real-life situations. For example, discussing current events or social issues can help children learn how to analyze complex situations and make informed decisions.

Additionally, it's important for parents and teachers to recognize the limits of children's ability in this stage. While they have the ability to think abstractly, they still need guidance and support in applying their critical thinking skills to new situations. By encouraging children to reflect on their own thought processes, they can learn to identify when they need additional information or help and seek it out.

Key Takeaways on the Formal Operational Stage:

THE FORMAL OPERATIONAL Stage is the fourth and final stage in Jean Piaget's theory of cognitive development, characterized by the development of abstract, logical, and hypothetical thinking.

During this stage, individuals are able to think logically about abstract concepts and consider multiple perspectives, making them capable of considering possibilities and making predictions about the future.

Formal operational thinking enables individuals to engage in scientific and mathematical reasoning, as well as engage in more complex problem-solving and decision-making.

Piaget believed that this stage occurs in adolescence and adulthood, and that not all individuals may reach this stage of development.

Some of the key limitations of formal operational thinking include egocentric thinking, where individuals may struggle to understand the perspectives of others, and difficulty considering multiple solutions to complex problems.

Despite these limitations, the development of formal operational thinking is considered a key milestone in human development, allowing individuals to engage in more complex and abstract thinking, and to reason logically about the world around them.

III. The Role of Schemas and Assimilation and Accommodation

J ean Piaget's theory of cognitive development proposed that children actively construct their understanding of the world through a continuous process of assimilation and accommodation. These two concepts are central to Piaget's theory and play a crucial role in how children learn and adapt to new experiences. In this section, we will delve into the role of schemas and explore how assimilation and accommodation work together to shape a child's understanding of the world.

A. Definition of schemas

A schema is a mental representation or framework that organizes and categorizes information about the world. For example, a child may have a schema for a dog that includes characteristics such as four legs, fur, and a wagging tail. When a child encounters a new dog, they can assimilate this information into their existing schema, making minor modifications if necessary. However, if the child encounters a dog with three legs, they will need to accommodate their schema to incorporate this new information. Through a constant process of assimilation and accommodation, children are able to construct and refine their understanding of the world around them.

B. Mechanisms of assimilation and accommodation

Assimmilation

Assimilation is a fundamental aspect of Jean Piaget's theory of cognitive development. According to Piaget, assimilation refers to the process by which individuals take in new information and experiences and integrate them into their existing knowledge structures, or schemas. This process is a natural part of human cognitive development and plays a critical role in shaping our understanding of the world around us.

Assimilation occurs when new information is incorporated into our existing schemas without necessarily changing those schemas. For example, if a child has a schema for dogs that includes the belief that all dogs have fur, they may see a picture of a hairless dog and still consider it to be a dog because they are able to assimilate the new information into their existing schema. This allows individuals to understand new information and experiences in the context of their existing knowledge, making it easier to process and remember the information.

The process of assimilation is particularly important in the early stages of cognitive development, as children are still building their schemas and developing their understanding of the world. In these early stages, children are more likely to engage in assimilation because their schemas are still relatively flexible and open to new information. However, as children grow and their schemas become more complex, they may begin to rely more on accommodation, which is the process of modifying existing schemas to fit new information.

Accommodation

ACCOMMODATION IS AN important concept in Jean Piaget's theory of cognitive development, and refers to the process by which an individual adjusts their understanding of the world in light of new information. The concept of accommodation is closely tied to the idea of schemas, which are mental frameworks that we use to organize and categorize information. When a person encounters information that does not fit within their existing schemas, they must accommodate it by modifying or creating a new schema to incorporate the new information.

Accommodation is a crucial part of Piaget's theory, as it helps explain how individuals continue to develop and refine their understanding of the world as they grow and gain more experience. It is an adaptive process that allows individuals to respond to changing situations and new information, and to make sense of their experiences in a meaningful way.

One of the key features of accommodation is that it is often accompanied by conflict and disequilibrium. This is because when new information does not fit within a person's existing schemas, it can create a sense of discomfort or confusion. This discomfort can motivate the person to modify their understanding of the world and make accommodations that allow them to better fit the new information.

Accommodation also plays a role in Piaget's stages of cognitive development, as it is an important factor in the transition from one stage to the next. As individuals continue to accommodate new information and experiences, they can reach higher levels of cognitive development and gain a more sophisticated understanding of the world.

Assimilation and accommodation are two sides of the same coin, and both play important roles in shaping our understanding of the world. By assimilating new information into our existing schemas, we are able to understand and make sense of new experiences and concepts. However, when assimilation is not possible, accommodation is necessary in order to update and refine our schemas to better reflect reality.

C. The importance of equilibration in cognitive development

The process of equilibration is an integral part of Jean Piaget's theory of cognitive development. According to Piaget, equilibration refers to the balancing of the conflicting forces of assimilation and accommodation, which are the building blocks of cognitive growth. The concept of equilibration highlights the idea that cognitive development is not a linear process, but rather an ongoing cycle of adaptation and readjustment.

Equilibration is what allows a child to integrate new experiences and information into their existing cognitive structures, or schemas. These schemas are mental frameworks that help us to organize and make sense of our experiences. When a new experience or piece of information contradicts our current schema, it can cause a state of disequilibrium, or an imbalance in our understanding. This disequilibrium can be resolved through accommodation, which involves adjusting our existing schema to accommodate the new information.

However, accommodation can only occur if assimilation is also taking place. Assimilation refers to the process of incorporating new information into our existing schemas without having to change them. This allows us to understand and make sense of new experiences without having to completely revise our understanding of the world. When both assimilation and accommodation are in balance, we reach a state of equilibrium, where our schemas are updated to accurately reflect our experiences.

The process of equilibration is an ongoing cycle that occurs throughout our lives. As we encounter new experiences and information, we must constantly adapt our schemas to accommodate them while also assimilating them into our existing understanding. This process allows us to develop a more accurate and nuanced understanding of the world around us.

Key takeaways

Jean Piaget's theory of cognitive development proposed that children actively construct their understanding of the world through a continuous process of assimilation and accommodation.

- Schemas are cognitive frameworks that guide our understanding and interpretation of the world around us.
- Assimilation occurs when new information is incorporated into our existing schemas, allowing us to understand and process it more easily.
- Accommodation occurs when our existing schemas are modified or adapted in order to make sense of new information that doesn't fit our existing understanding.
- Equilibration, the balance between assimilation and accommodation, is crucial for cognitive development and helps drive the progression through Piaget's stages of development.
- Schemas, assimilation, and accommodation play a vital role in how we make sense of new information and how our understanding of the world evolves over time.

IV. Criticisms of Piaget's Theory

Jean Piaget's theory of cognitive development has been widely studied and discussed in the field of psychology for over a century. While Piaget's work has made significant contributions to our understanding of child development and learning, it is not without its criticisms. In this section, we will explore some of the criticisms of Piaget's theory and examine how they have influenced the field of developmental psychology.

Cultural biases

In Piaget's theory of cognitive development, the stages of development are said to be universal and applicable to all individuals. However, there have been criticisms that Piaget's theory is limited in its recognition of cultural biases.

One of the main criticisms is that Piaget's theory does not take into account the different ways in which cultures and genders may influence cognitive development. Piaget's theory primarily focuses on the cognitive development of European and North American children, disregarding the experiences of children from other cultural backgrounds.

Research has found that Piaget's stages of development may not accurately reflect the experiences of children from non-European and non-North American cultures. For example, some cultures place a strong emphasis on interdependence and collectivism, which may result in a different pattern of cognitive development. Furthermore, some research has shown that children from certain cultures may develop their reasoning skills differently than children from other cultures, and that girls and boys may also have different patterns of development.

Gender biases

According to Piaget's theory, boys are more advanced in their cognitive development compared to girls. This is based on the idea that boys are more active and exploratory, which is seen as an indicator of cognitive development. However, this idea is not supported by recent research, which has shown that there are no gender differences in cognitive development.

Girls and boys both experience cognitive development in the same ways and at the same rates, but they may express it differently. For example, girls may be more nurturing and cooperative, while boys may be more competitive and adventurous. However, this does not mean that one gender is more advanced in their cognitive development compared to the other.

It is important to recognize that gender does play a role in the way children develop, but it is not the sole determining factor. Other factors, such as the child's environment and upbringing, can also have a significant impact on their cognitive development. For example, a child who grows up in a supportive and encouraging environment will likely develop better cognitive skills compared to a child who grows up in a neglectful or abusive environment.

Limited consideration of socio-economic factors

The theory is often viewed as being overly centered on the individual child, with limited recognition of the impact of wider cultural and social factors on cognitive development. This has led to criticism that Piaget's theory fails to fully appreciate the diversity of ways in which children learn and grow, and is therefore limited in its ability to provide a comprehensive understanding of the complexities of human cognition.

While Piaget acknowledged that environmental factors could play a role in the development of intelligence, he believed that these factors were secondary to the internal processes of assimilation and accommodation. Critics of his theory argue that this limited consideration of social and economic factors doesn't fully capture the complexity of cognitive development.

For example, research has shown that children from low-income families are often exposed to fewer cognitively stimulating experiences, which can negatively impact their cognitive development. Similarly, cultural factors, such as language and cultural practices, can play a significant role in shaping how children understand and interact with the world.

Additionally, research has shown that economic resources can greatly impact children's educational experiences, and in turn their cognitive development. For example, children from lower-income families are more likely to attend schools with fewer resources, which can lead to disparities in educational achievement and opportunities.

Fixed stages of development

According to Piaget, children progress through a set of universal and invariant stages, each marked by a particular type of thinking and way of understanding the world. However, many experts in the field of cognitive development argue that this view is too narrow and fails to account for the wide range of individual differences in the way that people develop expertise.

Critics argue that the development of expertise is much more complex and dynamic than Piaget's theory suggests. For example, some individuals may develop expertise in a particular domain much earlier or later than others, and some may skip stages altogether. Moreover, the development of expertise is often influenced by a wide range of factors, including motivation, opportunity, instruction, and practice.

Limited consideration of emotional factors

While Piaget's theory primarily focuses on the cognitive processes involved in development, it has been argued that emotions play a significant role in shaping a person's thinking and behavior. Emotions can influence a child's perception, attention, and memory, leading to different ways of understanding and responding to the world. They can also affect motivation and drive, influencing a child's behavior and willingness to learn and engage in new experiences.

Critics argue that by ignoring the emotional component of development, Piaget's theory oversimplifies the complex interplay between cognition and emotion. Moreover, by disregarding the impact of emotions, Piaget's theory does not fully capture the subjective and individual experiences of children. Emotional factors such as stress, anxiety, and trauma can have a profound impact on a child's cognitive and social development, and ignoring these factors limits our understanding of how children grow and change.

Limited explanation of the development of expertise

Another limitation of Piaget's theory is its limited explanation of the development of expertise. While the theory provides a comprehensive framework for the cognitive development of children in general, it does not provide a detailed explanation of how certain individuals become experts in a particular domain. For example, how do some children become expert musicians, while others do not? How do some children develop exceptional mathematical skills, while others struggle with basic arithmetic? Piaget's theory does not provide a clear explanation of these phenomena.

Key takeaways

Jean Piaget's cognitive development theory has been widely accepted and applied in various fields, including education, psychology, and sociology. However, his theory has also faced numerous criticisms over the years. Some of the key takeaways of these criticisms include:

- Limited Cultural and Gender Biases: Piaget's theory has been criticized for ignoring the impact of cultural and gender factors on cognitive development. Critics argue that Piaget's theory is Western-centric and that it doesn't consider the diversity of cognitive development in different cultures and gender.
- Limited Sociocultural Factors: The theory doesn't consider the role of social and economic factors in cognitive development. Critics argue that these factors play a significant role in shaping children's understanding of the world.
- Limited Consideration of Emotional Factors: Piaget's theory doesn't pay enough attention to the role of emotions in cognitive development. Critics argue that emotions play a crucial role in shaping children's perception of the world.
- Limited Explanation of Expertise Development: Piaget's theory provides a limited explanation of how children develop expertise in specific areas. Critics argue that the theory doesn't account for the acquisition of skills and knowledge in different domains, such as math, music, or sports.
- Fixed Stages of Development: Piaget's theory suggests that children go through fixed stages of development, which have

been criticized for being too rigid. Critics argue that the stages of development are not always as distinct and predictable as Piaget suggested.

V. Applications of Piaget's Theory

Jean Piaget's theory of cognitive development has had a profound impact on the field of psychology, education and beyond. His ideas on how children's thinking changes and evolves over time have been widely accepted and continue to be the subject of research and study. However, the significance of Piaget's theory extends far beyond the academic realm, and its applications can be seen in a variety of fields and settings. In this section, we will explore some of the key ways in which Piaget's ideas are being used to inform and improve educational practices, to understand the development of expertise, and to support children and young people as they navigate their way through the complexities of the world around them. From the classroom to the clinic, Piaget's theory has much to offer in terms of understanding and supporting the development of children and young people.

A. Education and Instruction

The theory of cognitive development proposed by Jean Piaget has had a significant impact on the field of education. Piaget's insights into the way children think and learn have been applied in various educational settings to improve teaching methods and student learning outcomes.

One of the key takeaways from Piaget's theory is the idea that children's cognitive abilities develop in stages, and that each stage is characterized by a distinct way of thinking. This understanding of the development of thought has allowed educators to tailor their teaching methods to the specific cognitive abilities of their students. For example, in the preoperational stage, where children are still learning to think logically and systematically, teachers may focus on hands-on activities and concrete examples to help children understand abstract concepts.

Another important aspect of Piaget's theory is the role of experience and interaction in cognitive development. Piaget believed that children actively construct their understanding of the world through their experiences and interactions with their environment. This idea has been applied in educational settings through the use of hands-on activities, group work, and problem-based learning, which provide students with opportunities to interact with their environment and construct their own understanding of concepts.

Piaget's theory has also been applied in the development of educational materials, such as textbooks and educational software. By considering the cognitive abilities and thought processes of different age groups, educational materials can be designed to be more effective in teaching specific concepts and skills.

Finally, Piaget's theory has had a significant impact on our understanding of the importance of play in children's development. Piaget believed that play was an essential aspect of cognitive development, allowing children to explore and experiment with their environment in a safe and controlled way. This understanding has led to an emphasis on play-based learning in early childhood education, where children are encouraged to play and explore in order to develop their cognitive and social skills.

B. Child Development and Parenting

Piaget's theory of cognitive development has far-reaching implications for understanding child development and for parenting. Understanding Piaget's stages of development can help parents and caregivers to better understand the mental and emotional development of children, and to adapt their approaches accordingly.

One of the key insights of Piaget's theory is the recognition that children at different stages of development have different cognitive capabilities. For example, a child in the preoperational stage may struggle with complex problem-solving and cause-and-effect relationships, while a child in the formal operational stage is capable of abstract reasoning and hypothesis testing. Understanding these developmental differences can help parents to better understand their child's behavior, and to provide appropriate support and guidance.

Another important aspect of Piaget's theory is the recognition of the importance of hands-on exploration and experimentation in the development of knowledge and understanding. Children learn best through direct experience, and it is through this kind of exploration that they construct their own mental representations of the world around them. Parents and caregivers can support this process by providing children with a wide range of opportunities for play and exploration, and by encouraging them to think critically about their experiences.

Moreover, Piaget's theory highlights the role of interaction and cooperation in cognitive development. Children learn from the interactions they have with others, and from observing and imitating the behaviors of others. Parents can encourage this process by engaging in meaningful interactions with their children, and by creating a supportive and cooperative family environment.

C. Cognitive Assessment and Intervention

One of the most important applications of Piaget's theory in cognitive assessment and intervention is the development of stage-specific assessment tools. Piaget's stages of development provide a framework for understanding the typical cognitive development of children. This has been used to create age-specific assessments that can help identify areas of strength and weakness in a child's thinking and problem-solving abilities. For example, assessments that are designed for children in the concrete operational stage will focus on tasks that assess their ability to think logically and solve problems based on their understanding of physical properties.

Another application of Piaget's theory in this field is the development of interventions aimed at supporting the cognitive development of children. For example, if a child is found to be lagging behind in their cognitive development, interventions can be designed to help them build their understanding and skills in specific areas. This might include activities that encourage children to engage in hands-on exploration and discovery, or the use of educational games and puzzles that challenge their thinking and problem-solving abilities.

Additionally, Piaget's theory has been used to inform the design of educational materials and programs for children. For example, educational materials that are appropriate for children in the preoperational stage might include activities and games that encourage children to develop their imagination and language skills. Materials for children in the concrete operational stage might focus on teaching them logical thinking and problem-solving skills.

Key takeaways

Piaget's theory of cognitive development has a number of applications in various fields, including education, child development and parenting, and cognitive assessment and intervention.

In Education: Piaget's theory has been widely used in the field of education to design developmentally appropriate learning experiences for students at different stages of cognitive development.

Child development and parenting: Piaget's theory provides insights into a child's cognitive development, helping parents and caregivers to better understand their child's thought processes and provide appropriate support and guidance.

Cognitive Assessment and Intervention: Piaget's theory informs cognitive assessment and intervention practices, allowing practitioners to identify and address cognitive difficulties at different stages of development.

Understanding individual differences: Piaget's theory also highlights the importance of considering individual differences in cognitive development and the impact of environmental factors.

Limitations: While Piaget's theory has provided valuable insights into cognitive development, it has faced criticism for its limitations in explaining the role of emotions, cultural and gender biases, and the development of expertise.

Interdisciplinary Approach: Piaget's theory is best applied in an interdisciplinary approach, taking into account other theories and findings from fields such as psychology, neuroscience, and education.

VI. Conclusion

In the world of developmental psychology, Piaget's theory of cognitive development remains one of the most influential and widely studied ideas of the 20th century. Despite its criticism, Piaget's theory has provided a foundation for understanding how children develop their cognitive abilities and how they come to understand the world around them. Through his extensive research, Piaget identified four distinct stages of cognitive development, each marked by a unique set of cognitive abilities and ways of thinking. He also theorized the concept of schemas and the processes of assimilation and accommodation, as well as the concept of equilibration, which helps explain how children seek balance and stability in their cognitive development.

As we come to the conclusion of this discussion, it is important to summarize the key points and takeaways from Piaget's theory of cognitive development. From its contribution to our understanding of child development and its applications in education and child assessment, Piaget's theory continues to shape the way we think about the growth of the human mind.

A. Summary of Key Points

In conclusion, Piaget's theory of cognitive development remains a significant contribution to the field of psychology and education. This theory provides a framework for understanding how children think and learn, and it offers insights into the processes that drive cognitive growth.

The theory posits that children pass through four distinct stages of cognitive development: the sensorimotor stage, the preoperational stage, the concrete operational stage, and the formal operational stage. Each stage is marked by specific cognitive skills and abilities, and the transition from one stage to the next is characterized by changes in how children think, reason, and understand the world around them.

Piaget's theory also highlights the importance of schemas and the ways in which they guide children's thinking and learning. Schemas are mental structures that help children organize and make sense of new information, and they play a central role in both assimilation and accommodation. These two processes work together to maintain cognitive balance and drive cognitive growth.

The theory has been criticized for its limited attention to cultural and gender biases, as well as for its lack of attention to emotional and social factors in development. Despite these limitations, Piaget's theory has been applied in a variety of ways, including in the fields of education, child development and parenting, and cognitive assessment and intervention.

In summary, Piaget's theory provides a valuable foundation for understanding the cognitive development of children, and it continues to play a significant role in shaping our understanding of how children think, learn, and grow.

B. Reflection on the legacy and continued relevance of Piaget's Theory of Cognitive Development

In the field of psychology, Jean Piaget's theory of cognitive development has left a lasting legacy. The theory, which proposes that children actively construct their understanding of the world through their experiences and interactions, has had a profound impact on our understanding of how children think and learn. Nearly a century after its introduction, Piaget's theory continues to be highly influential and relevant.

One of the key contributions of Piaget's theory is the emphasis it places on the active role of the child in their own development. Unlike previous theories, which saw children as passive recipients of knowledge, Piaget recognized that children are constantly exploring and constructing their own understanding of the world. This view has had a profound impact on our understanding of how children learn, and has informed the development of more child-centered approaches to education.

Another important aspect of Piaget's theory is its focus on the development of thought processes. Piaget proposed that children go through four distinct stages of development, each characterized by a different level of cognitive ability. While some aspects of this theory have been criticized, the stages of development still provide a useful framework for understanding the key cognitive changes that take place during childhood.

Despite its many contributions, Piaget's theory is not without its limitations. For example, some have criticized the theory for its limited consideration of cultural and gender factors, and for its limited explanation of the development of expertise. However, these criticisms have largely been incorporated into more recent theories, which build upon and expand upon Piaget's ideas.

Don't miss out!

Visit the website below and you can sign up to receive emails whenever Dr. Milos Kankaras publishes a new book. There's no charge and no obligation.

https://books2read.com/r/B-A-LEAZ-AZMKC

BOOKS 2 READ

Connecting independent readers to independent writers.

Also by Dr. Milos Kankaras

A Simple Guide

Lev Vygotsky's Theory of Cognitive Development: A Simple Guide

Standalone

Jean Piaget's Theory of Cognitive Development: A Simple Guide

Watch for more at https://oecd.academia.edu/MilošKankaraš.

About the Author

Dr Miloš Kankaraš is an experienced policy analyst, project manager and author with a rich track record in providing an empirical foundation for evidence-based public policy in international settings. He worked in academia before moving to some of the leading international organisations, where he examined issues ranging from education, skill development, social policy, working conditions, gender equality, quality of life, etc. Miloš published extensively in a variety of policy and research areas. He has an undergraduate degree in Psychology, graduate degrees in educational psychology and international social policy, and a PhD in the area of cross-cultural research.